7 SIMPLE STRATEGIES

FOR

OUTSTANDING LEADERSHIP

ERIC HARDING WALKER

Published by:

Hardwalk, LLC
PO Box 27256
Scottsdale, Arizona 85255-5144

FIRST EDITION
Printed in USA
ISBN 978-0-692-07819-8

$16.99
ISBN 978-0-692-07819-8
51699>

9 780692 078198

Acknowledgements

Thank you to my parents for providing my life with sustenance, strength, encouragement and the understanding that without setbacks and challenges success can never be measured.

Table of Contents

Why Leadership

In the early years of the founding of the United States, the newly established settlements felt a need to separate themselves from British rule for a variety of unique reasons. It was clear that each group would benefit from freedom, but there was no unity between the settlements. This lack of unity, direction, and focus initially helped the British to maintain control over the new colonies, and to continue to profit from the trade and commerce the settlers were engaged.

This all changed once the founding fathers began to enlist strong leaders who had a clear focus on freedom from British rule. As the founding fathers created a structure and process to set up a sophisticated network of intelligence, the British began to recognize the settlements as a formidable opposition to the crown, and a legitimate force in the new world. It was the undeniable leadership of the founding fathers that was the driving force for the United States of America to become a free nation.

Leadership is a necessary part of society. Anytime there are people who have a common goal, you will find leadership. It is of the utmost importance in our culture. Any organization, group, club, association, or company function based upon the leadership in place.

Leadership is a behavior that occurs naturally in almost all formal and informal social situations. Even among our friends, group leaders will emerge with time. There are always people in our inner circles who take on the leadership role; managing the carpool dues, organizing a fantasy sports league, or deciding 'who should bring what' to the annual church potluck.

While there may be subtle differences in personality that help define a 'leader' in a particular group, the spirit that drives these individuals can be found in everyone.

Leadership is not simply a title. It does not always come with power. Leadership can often be a pattern of behaviors; an approach of 'modeling,' where actions speak louder than words. Mastery of leadership as a behavior that leverages influence with people, as opposed to a rank and file relationship, is a necessary skill for any true leader.

Leadership is important to life, a universal system of communication that helps things get done. Without leadership, chaos would reign and the world would descend into uncertainty; with doubt and confusion becoming the norm. At its core, leadership helps mankind forge ahead, against insurmountable odds.

Remember too, that with leadership comes great responsibility. Trust carries emotional connections, and relationships should not be taken lightly. Those who are power hungry will ultimately fail as leaders, driven by motivations which cannot coexist in harmony with true leadership. Money, fame, and power can be side effects of leadership – but leaders who focus on the attainment of these will ultimately become dictators.

If you truly are interested in leadership, allow the process to evolve naturally. Preparation is key, focus and determination are recommended. In the end, true leadership is within us all – but it must be understood to be effective. With patience and time, if you so desire, you will begin to exhibit the characteristics of a great leader.

"A leader...is like a shepherd. He stays behind the flock, letting the most nimble go out ahead, whereupon the others follow, not realizing that all along they are being directed from behind."
– Nelson Mandela

Lessons of Leadership

George nervously clutched three white envelopes. As the newly appointed CEO he was about to meet with the company Board for the first time. His predecessor–a well seasoned executive–had warned him that the Board could be difficult to manage. He was nervous and apprehensive, but he was also determined to be successful in his new leadership role.

George knew the outgoing CEO well. The two had spent time together both on and off the job. The prior CEO had been a good leader – but after several quarters of poor company earnings he had resigned.

On his last day the CEO reached out to George and asked him to join him in his office. "George," he said, "I hope you learned from me and will be ready to step into the role of CEO." The newly resigned CEO then smiled at George, shook his hand and gave him three envelopes numbered #1, #2, and #3.

"If you ever find yourself in a tough situation with the Board you will find all the advice you need in these three envelopes." George quickly tucked them into the pocket of his notebook, thanked the former CEO for his advice, and left the office.

The next couple of months were a whirlwind of activity. George had been busy – learning about the company, making some key decisions, and attempting to support the company goals. The envelopes were far removed from his mind.

As he had his first meeting with the Board, he was assailed by complaints about poor company performance, lack of new market growth, and poor company strategy. Without attracting attention, George gently slid the envelope labeled '#1' out of his notebook and opened it. He was shocked by its message:

"Blame Your Predecessor"

George felt uncomfortable with the message. As the Board complained about the current state of affairs, he wondered if there was a diplomatic way to blame the former CEO. While it was certainly not ideal, it did seem like the perfect way to distance himself from his predecessor's style of management, and give him some time to make any necessary adjustments. George decided to speak up, and he proceeded to tell the Board that many of the company's challenges were due to the foundation that had been put in place prior to his arrival. He assured them that he would dedicate the next few months to putting the organization back on a pathway for success.

As days and weeks passed, not many things went as planned, and George soon found himself sitting again with an unhappy Board. This time, the Board was frustrated with a lack of accountability and decreasing profits. Discouraged by the Board's impatience and continued bickering about the state of affairs in the organization, he pulled out the second envelope, labeled #2, unfolding the paper to see what it said:

"Launch a re-organization plan"

As he thought about the idea, George wondered if such a thing could work. He knew that things needed to change, and he had ideas about how the organization could be more efficient – there were ways staff could be more responsive to members, donors, and supporters.

Over many weeks, he had reviewed policies, analyzed service statistics, and scoured organization charts to uncover issues, and figure out where and why things were going wrong. Maybe this is exactly what the company needs—a reorganization.

At the next meeting, with a renewed sense of purpose and a fresh plan in hand, he stepped forward to announce plans for a re-organization. Staff would be re-assigned. Redundant positions would be eliminated. New programs would be launched. A fresh direction was ready to be implemented.

His plan was greeted with open arms. George felt so much better. Of course he would still have to prove he could deliver, but at least he had calmed the Board and he had a path forward.

Determined to propel the organization, he set about the hard work of leading change. He worked closely with staff, helping them re-orient themselves to the new plan. He re-defined their roles, and focused them on the tough tasks of improving member service. Prospecting and acquiring new members was now a priority. Finding new value and innovations among the varied services and products offered by the group became a key activity. While the team appeared engaged, it was clear this was a long-term strategy, and would require both dedication and sharp focus in the face of so much change.

With the next meeting now just a few weeks away, George was again nervous and anxious. The entire team had made progress and member service satisfaction was improving. Service costs had fallen, but the organization was still struggling to re-define itself.

Committee leaders were voicing complaints about changed priorities. A few had even taken to communicating by e-mail directly with the Board. In a few instances the Board met with team members to discuss "behind the scenes" activities of the organization. Incomplete information had led to perceptions of failure.

Preparing to join the Board meeting, George grabbed his portfolio and headed to the gathering. The meeting did not go well. Several

Board members publicly shared complaints they had heard from team members. After much back and forth, the Board revealed the extensive "behind the scenes" communications and complaints received.

As the meeting wore on, the discussions grew more contentious with some of the Board supporting George and the change efforts, and others discounting that any progress had been made. As he continued to listen to the discussions and take rapid-fire notes, the envelope marked "#3" slipped from behind the pocket in his portfolio.

The room was abuzz with chatter—accusations, counter accusations, fault-finding, rich opinions, and endless discussions about what to do. George, seeking a respite from the conversations and inspiration in the moment, decided to open the third envelope. Slowly, he unfolded the paper hoping to find a message of guidance.

Gradually, a smile spread across his face. Neatly typed in the center of the page was one sentence. It read:

"Make Out Three Envelopes"

Outstanding leadership is an awe-inspiring characteristic. It is a trait of one's personality that is not simply inherited, and leadership is often perfected over time, through trial and error. For many people, when thinking of desirable traits, leadership ranks near the top of the list. And rightfully so – because great leaders have conquered lands, built civilizations, and shaped the world as we know it. Leadership is a crucial part of the human experience.

So who are these leaders and what do they do differently? Well, truth be told, it's not that easy to define. There are many kinds of leaders in this world. There are past leaders who have shaped our history and future leaders who have yet to make their mark on society. Leaders come from all walks of life; and, in turn, they have various approaches to leadership. But all outstanding leaders share a common trait; a common polarity that seems to tie them together.

While not an exact science or metric, it's clear that leaders do everything, whether good or bad, with uncompromising values, unbreakable focus, and a penchant for success. They all possess a kind of unique and highly developed skillset for building relationships, communicating idea, and innovation that helps them perform where others fail.

Outstanding leadership is a unique skillset. While leadership is in high demand, it is outstanding leadership which is coveted. So what is the difference between the two types of leadership? Normal leadership is easy to excecute. It is the next level – outstanding leadership – which is the elusive prize so highly sought after.

The characteristics of outstanding leadership are difficult to find. Like a precious gemstone, it can hide in plain sight, and finding it can be both time-consuming and challenging.

Once found, the reward is great – but still requires effort.

Imagine a raw, uncut diamond. While the value may lie in the pure carat size, it can be said that the final product inclusive of color, cut, and clarity all add the overall value. So, as with leadership, the raw stone still requires work – effort from a seasoned craftsman to cut and carve the final, polished gemstone we call a diamond. Finding leaders is hard, and once found the transition to an outstanding leader is like the polishing of a diamond.

People often say that, 'Great leaders are everywhere, but so are bad leaders.' This characterizes the challenge of finding true leaders – the ones willing to develop the skillset required to become an outstanding leader. There are many who are willing to lead – those who have the basic raw talent, skillset, and qualifications. Yet these raw leaders lack the final, polished product.

Leaders who have the unique ability to lead despite all odds, through times of tumultuous change, against all odds with unwavering belief and conviction are the outstanding leaders who become the diamonds we know and admire.

Finding outstanding leadership for an organization can be a time-consuming process. The search will usually create a constant churn of team members who can lead as instructed – but who fail at delivering the next level of performance.

This happens because many believe that leadership is represented by a title or tenure. The idea that outstanding leaders should have a higher level of performance is irrelevant. While many would assume that this next level of performance is measured by employee engagement and optimism, is often times simply measured in corner offices and nameplates.

The idea that a leader should be responsible to engage, motivate and drive innovation becomes a distant hope - usually relegated only to those fortunate companies like Apple or Google, who continually seem to attract and retain the most gifted employees.

To prove this idea, think of a management title you have in your organization. A director, for example, is someone who is in charge of an activity, department or organization. A Director can usually be referred to as the manager responsible for overseeing the actions and affairs of a business line or unit. As such, the Director is typically given heavy authority. Not only must that person manage the day to day operations of a profit center, but also engage teams and ensure performance. Does any of that require outstanding leadership?

Most organizations would agree that within the capacity of a Director role, a person would be required to display some, if not all, outstanding leadership qualities. But in reality, that is rarely the case. Many mid to senior level managers are well short of outstanding leadership – and to no fault of their own. They have simply been moved up the ladder, one rung at a time, and are ok getting by in the new role – adapting as they go along.

This is a common problem in companies. There are often times where managers have been moved along the conveyor belt of restructures, realignments, and mergers/acquisitions into leadership positions. This creates a unique dilemma for companies.

On one hand, it makes sense to align your most loyal and trusted advisors into key management roles. This provides consistency in messaging and shows that hard work can help you progress in your career. On the other hand, it calls into question whether or not the best resources are being committed to leading the teams. Often, organizations will combine both approaches, creating a blend that seems to align with the company goals.

The key takeaway for organizations to understand is simple. The more that companies can help differentiate characteristics of outstanding leaders from normal management, the better they will be at helping these same managers perform management duties. Once a company can determine which leaders are able to incorporate the entire blend of outstanding leadership skills the sooner the company can start having candid conversations around performance and strategy.

This constant ebb and flow between management and leadership creates a leadership paradox. It is in a company's best interest to find leaders that inspire, motivate, and help grow its bottom line. These leaders are essential for success. They will become the catalysts necessary to move the performance needle from 99 to 100.

Without the leaders, we will maintain status quo – never developing beyond our initial burst of growth. We will flounder in the confusion and paralysis analyses of mismanagement and poor alignment. The mission is simple, yet it is most critical to building a strong foundation: find highly talented and inspiring leaders that can help propel your vision into action.

You may ask: "Is the leadership paradox really a problem?" The simple answer is: 'It depends.' We all know that people with an ability to lead, aka 'leaders,' are in high demand. Once you find them, they are being quickly lured away by competitors with lucrative offers and challenging opportunities.

Leaders who were once happy and engaged are now looking for new horizons to flex their leadership prowess - and are anticipating commensurate compensation. Ultimately, these leaders will move on, and those who come in to fill the ranks may not possess the leadership skills of their prior counterparts.

It may be that these people who have now progressed to a senior role are great Directors – and nothing more. And while it is not entirely wrong, these people are not the same team you want at your table making decisions about how to execute strategy and develop vision. But often times, they are, and so the shuffle begins anew.

In order to find an outstanding leader, it is important to think like one. Think about the rare leader you may have encountered in the past. Was it the title that inspired you? What was the special thing that this person did to make you think of them today? How did this person manage to make a significant impact, one that we remember? What did they do that makes us want to share the lesson with our children, our colleagues, our friends?

Outstanding leadership cannot be contained within a box. It's not a specific metric. There isn't a standard formula. There is no path you can follow that will lead to ultimate leadership wisdom. Leaders come from all walks of life. Some are wealthy and some are not, some have never attended college and others have studied with the world's leading scholars. So, how do we begin to understand what makes a leader 'outstanding'? Where do we begin to draw the line?

Outstanding leadership is an amalgamation of qualities. The secret blend combines characteristics we all possess, but rarely call upon. One example of a common trait shared by outstanding leaders is that they tend to keep things simple. They focus on how to make a difference for everyone around them… making things better for others.

If you want to be a successful leader, then make life better for those around you. Focusing on the needs of others, truly understanding the challenges faced by others is unique to outstanding leadership.

So, to be clear, outstanding leadership is not a simple task. If it were an easy task we would all rise to be great leaders, and no one would have purchased this book. But in all honesty, not everyone wants to be a leader. There are plenty of people who are content to participate and contribute. There are also many who believe they are outstanding leaders, but are really only average. The path to becoming an outstanding leader is one that requires hard work and dedication. It's a difficult challenge for the best and brightest, and can be a lonely path of self discovery. As Robert Frost once said: 'I took the one less traveled by, and that has made all the difference.'

For the person who takes this path, the rewards are great. There is self discovery – you learn a lot about yourself, about whom and what you are. There is the connection – reaching out to others and making friendships that can last a lifetime. There can be true respect and admiration – people recognize your abilities, and look to you as the subject matter expert.

There are many benefits, and each journey to leadership will ultimately be unique. But the characteristics you develop, the skills you gain, and the abilities you share will be very similar to the greatest leaders who have come before, and of those that will follow.

Ultimately, leadership in any form is about making a difference. Judgement of your abilities to lead will be derived from the change you are able to make. This will be the true proof that your path to leadership was indeed the right one. As said before, each path is unique. Some leaders want to be able to make positive changes in people's lives, and so in this regard, these leaders are very selfless people. Some leaders will devote time and energy to leading teams and reaching consensus. They may be viewed as very collaborative leaders.

Regardless of the path chosen, each leader faces difficult obstacles – each path is challenging and complex. Leaders require discipline, strategy, commitment, and continual management in order to be successful. Leadership is a 24/7, 365 day endeavor. It never sleeps.

The path of leadership is a long journey, filled with setbacks and discouragements along the way. But outstanding leaders embrace the challenge, and seek to make a difference. These leaders are the ones that run towards the goal when others run away. They look to build upon previous knowledge, and share in the findings. To an outstanding leader, the idea that simple execution of strategy and delivery of requirements on a consistent basis are what determines a good leader is flawed. They know that leaders are so much more.

Sometimes, we feel that leadership is a right – it can be handed down by rank, bloodline, or mandate. While these are all ways that leaders can be created, it is not an accurate picture of outstanding leadership. To assume that outstanding leadership is granted via special powers or that it is somehow a designation given to those who seem worthy, is false. Imagine if we could just give wings to pilots, or badges to police officers. It is inaccurate to say that leaders can be given anything. While titles may come, these will be lost if the leader is not willing to develop leadership behaviors and actions.

Leaders encourage, and they inspire. They listen to the sounds of progress, and they look toward the future with open eyes. An outstanding leader is someone who will not simply manage expectations, but will exceed them. The passion that leaders exude is transformed into energy, and this can be passed on throughout an organization. It is a powerful force.

If you are reading this book, you have taken the first step towards becoming an outstanding leader. Willingness to understand that there are always areas for improvement is the gateway to transformation. Becoming an outstanding leader requires practice, hard work, and an open mind. If you are willing to take a chance with new ideas, you are not afraid of failure, and you believe in selflessly serving others, then the opportunity to become an outstanding leader exists in you.

Today you have started on a new journey. Embrace it, enjoy it, and do your best. Remember, everyone falls down – only those who get back up will succeed.

Eric

Leaders Help Others Find Inner Purpose

There is importance in understanding what lies beneath, the hidden soul and passion that yearns to be set free. Finding inner truth is the first page in the novel of a glorious life.

At the turn of the century, there was a very successful factory owner named Thomas Jones. Jones had built an empire offering high quality products at reasonable prices. Jones was well known and respected in the community he served.

Jones was getting older, and had begun the process of turning the company over to his son. The son was eager to learn the business, and his father was eager to share his craft. Jones' hope was that one day his son would succeed him in leading the company.

Because the company was very large and had complex inner workings, Jones had devised a training regimen for his son that culminated with a short apprenticeship with a family friend, who was also the Vice President of a large division within the company.

One day the Vice President informed Jones that his son had successfully completed his apprenticeship, but had one final test to pass. The Vice President went on to explain to Jones that the final test would take place the following week, and that once completed, the son would be ready to take over the reigns as the company leader. Jones was ecstatic and shared the good news with his son. The son was elated with the news, and diligently began to prepare for his final test.

That Monday the son rushed to meet with the Vice President, who explained that while the final test would be difficult, it could be completed if he was truly ready to take over the reigns. The test, he said, would involve the son going to the factory floor recording all the important sounds he heard. The Vice President would then review the sounds, and give the young man his grade. The only acceptable grade would be earned if the son heard 100% of the sounds, but would have 3 tries. If after three attempts, the son was not able to hear all the sounds – he would be forced into a lower level position and not allowed to work in management.

The son sprang into action. "What an easy task," the son thought. "I know the company's inner workings by heart." The young man returned the following day with a list of all the sounds. "I heard grinders, press machines, and drills," he stated confidently.

The Vice President's reply stunned the son. "Unfortunately you did not hear everything. You do not pass. Would you like to try again?"
The son, with a puzzled look on his face, hastily replied, "Of course, I will do better this time."

The next day, the son began to listen again. He listened much harder this time, hearing metal crashing together and sparks hitting the factory floor. He made a note of everything, and felt very confident upon presenting the new list to the Vice President.

"I heard much more this time," stated the son, feeling extremely confident.
The Vice President quickly glanced at the list. Shaking his head, he replied, "You did hear more, but not everything. Try again?"
With a puzzled look, the desperate son replied,

"But there isn't anything more! I listened as hard as I could… it's all there on the paper!"
The VP calmly replied, "Try again?"
The son, anxious to please his father, agreed to his final attempt. But he was confused, and afraid he may not pass this test.
Before he could leave to take the third and final test, the Vice President pulled the son aside.

"Listen. Truly listen…do not simply hear," he said as the son walked out onto the factory floor.

"Listen?" thought the son. "I am listening!"

The son sat down on the factory floor, and listened as hard as he could. He still heard the drills, the metal, and the sparks. But then something happened. As he sat there listening, he began to hear the workers. They weren't speaking directly to him, but he could still hear them. Some talked about their kids, others about restless nights. A few worried about company layoffs, while others wondered about getting a raise. He heard frustrations as well as motivations, sorrow as well as joy. It was as if a cloud had been lifted. He understood the test.

The son ran to deliver his new list, and the Vice President smiled.

"To hear the unheard," remarked the Vice President, "is a necessary discipline to be a good leader. Only when a leader has learned to listen closely to the hearts of the employees can he hope to inspire confidence in his company. The demise of a company comes when leaders listen only to superficial words, and do not penetrate deeply into the souls of the people to hear their true opinions, feelings, and desires. Congratulations… you passed!"

The son went on to lead the company into its most profitable years, and when the time came he began to prepare his teenager for the same test.

Outstanding leaders are those who inspire great performances. They find common ground with mutual benefit, and are able to offer motivation through actions rather than demands.

This shifts the focus of conversation from the normal 'success vs. failure' mantra to one in which all parties involved leave the table feeling motivated and encouraged. This is known as a 'win-win' scenario – the key to any successful negotiation. This emphasis on a partnership rather than rank and file is derived from a belief that character, honesty, and truth are the ultimate measure of success for any relationship.

Outstanding leaders avoid creating environments where competition drives success. These environments of animosity or jealousy will most likely drive short-term success, but they can impact performance in the long-run. A better approach is to lead by example, and to find common ground – avoid calling out the gap between high and low, the best and the worst.

Competitive environments, a culture with an emphasis placed on the material reward, will have a similar outcome. It will divide leaders, teams, and individuals – causing communication challenges; parties will never feel like a 'win-win' relationship exists. The more that a leader rewards behavior with tokens of appreciation, the more that leader will actually divide.

This division quickly becomes a line in the sand. On a team, there are the haves and the have nots. To be successful, win at all cost, and make sure you 'have.' Otherwise, you become an obvious failure.

So, for those that do achieve success, such motivation becomes a constant quest for more acceptance from material gain; aka greed. For the others it becomes a constant reminder of their failures and subsequent non-acceptance.

Often leaders using this approach find that individuals become focused simply on gaining wealth, and will turn to shortcuts to perceived success. When your definition of leadership includes material success as a measurement, teams will risk all and lose everything in the process.

An alternative approach to performance-based leadership starts with incorporating a broader view of success. When evaluating performance, pay special attention to the various aspects of each individual's skillset. Remember that everyone has different abilities. It takes a team to win a game – each player contributes his/her talents to the roster.

As a leader, you must help bring out the best performance in each member of your team. Looking at a team through a holistic lens can help align goals, and drive towards a 'win-win' scenario for all parties involved. Your team will begin to share ideas and thoughts, and help create a natural synergy. We all know that we are more open to ideas when we are not avoiding being considered a failure.

Keep in mind, however, that style is not a substitute for substance. Helping bring out the best in an individual requires a laser focus – distractions will be present, and will require careful navigation to remain on course.

There are many individuals who are very knowledgeable, but are not able to apply any particular skillset. Outstanding leadership requires active participation from both sides – it will not work with individuals who do not engage.

For any person, regardless of education, there are pieces of knowledge that can only be learned through the experience of involvement.

Sometimes walking a mile will help the journey of one hundred miles. Outstanding leaders help others crawl before they walk – understanding that each step builds on the one before.

Individual accomplishment and recognition is important, but teams with a strong leader will recognize the importance of being an individual also means working toward the greater group synergy. As a person develops a clear sense of being, they find internal peace, and are able to share that with others. A constant fear of retribution, rating, and measurement can block individuals from growing – as they constantly look for the path of least resistance (negative feedback).

Outstanding leaders who lead from behind, helping individuals along a path of learning and self discovery, without fear of isolation and judgement, can reap huge rewards.

As a leader, work towards that mindset – growth vs. performance, team vs. individual, long-term vs. short-term. Remember that leadership is about helping each individual have their best performance.

Leaders Treat All As Equals

A common goal will only be common when there is unity. A leader is not a special character, but a contributing part. All parts must come together, on equal ground, for innovation to happen.

Before the land was settled, when it was still wild and free, there were mining towns scattered throughout the west. These towns were known for their lawless nature – where rule of law was no more than the quick draw of a gun. At the turn of the century it quickly became apparent that in order for our nation to grow and expand these towns would require law and order.

Several towns chose to enforce the rule of law with local government. Government was usually run by a newly-elected mayor, mainly imported from the east coast, whose primary job was to encourage citizens to engage in civilized activities – avoiding rustling, gambling, and prostitution. The mayor would used any means necessary, finding the lawless towns filled with corruption, and often turned to hired gunmen, who could enforce the laws with a deadlier approach.

This approach worked, towns would flourish with death being the punishment for breaking the law. But if a town wanted to incorporate and obtain federal funding they needed dissolve the widely publicized view of outlaw towns filled with poker, wine, and women.

One Mayor in particular was struggling to adopt the newer, more civilized rule of law. His approach - anyone in violation of law would spend a night in jail – was not making progress. It was actually having the opposite effect, causing confrontations with locals who were less than pleased with the new statutes.

Frustrated at his lack of success, the Mayor decided to seek out advice from a well-known Mountain man. This Mountain man, who had lived in the area long before gold was found, was said to be wise beyond his years, and was often sought out as a source of guidance.

The Mayor packed for the week-long ride, and started down the trail to where the Mountain man lived. It was a difficult ride, but it gave the Mayor time to think. As the day passed into night, he felt confident that the ride would be worthwhile – realizing that his days would be numbered if there were no answers at the end of the journey.

Once he arrived, he found the Mountain man returning from a successful hunt. He was drying beaver pelts on a large stone perch overlooking the valley. The Mayor quickly dismounted his horse, walked over and exchanged greetings. The Mayor quickly began to explain hi stroubles, but the gruff old Mountain Man was hesitant to offer any indication that advice might be forthcoming.

As the Mayor began to explain his dire situation, he carefully crafted his tale, explaining the details of how he was recruited to work in the town, and quickly established rule of law. He described his strong leadership style, and the setbacks he had faced. It was apparent to the Mountain Man that the Mayor was facing challenges, resulting in chaos and disorder. The Mayor admitted his confusion, and frustration with the situation.

The Mountain Man sighed. Rather than speak, he motioned to the horse, indicating that the Mayor prepare to ride off with him. The Mayor quickly jumped on his horse, and the two headed down a path deeper into the mountains.

After several hours of riding the Mountain Man stopped at a fork in the road by the Snake River. The river was wide and deep, and was difficult to cross – it was named 'snake' because it swayed like a long snake in the grass, winding its way down the mountain through the valley.

As the sun faded over the valley, the two of them spent the waning minutes of daylight watering the horses, setting up camp, and preparing a late meal. Sitting around the campfire the Mountain Man and Mayor admired the large flames that lit up the night sky. The fire burned brilliantly for hours, leaping against the sky, until the stars seemed dim.

When the Mayor woke the next morning, the sun had already begun to edge over the mountains, and the brilliant flame of the campfire was gone. After a quick breakfast, and cleanup of the campsite, the Mountain Man then turned the Mayor's attention to the river.

The Mountain Man gruffly asked, "Look at that here River. Not doin' much, I reckon. That'll put some good ideas in that coal bean head of yurs…"

The Mayor was confused. He did not understand at all. "I'm sorry," he said, puzzled. "I don't understand… the river? What does it mean?"

The Mountain Man cracked a wry smile. "Think," he said dryly, "about that fire from last night. It was strong, powerful, and pretty darn amazing. Heck, the flames were as tall as the night sky. I reckon nothing could have matched its heat. It would have destroyed anything that'd come 'cross its path."

He paused, furrowed his brow as if deep in thought. The Mayor patiently waited. The Mountain Man continued. "Now I reckon you think 'bout that river in front of you. The river starts out small as a baby deer, is mild-tempered, and calm. It slowly grows wide and becomes a force of nature. It don't happen overnight, the river follows a path, slow, and steady, breaking into every crack in the earth."

Here the Mountain Man paused, crouched low to the river, placing one finger over his lips to signal 'quiet' and his other hand into the water. "If you listen, you can barely hear it. Put your hand in the water, you can barely feel it."

He paused to smile. "So what's this tell you? Well, I figure it's like this. What's left of the fire? Ashes. That fire is so strong it destroys everything... even itself. On the other hand, the river will always be around."

The Mountain Man stood up, shaking his hand dry. "It's always flowing, broader and deeper, always more powerful along the journey to the end – providing a path for all."

The Mountain Man paused, and then continued."If there is one thing these mountains will teach you, it's that we are all the same. Nature, me, you – we are all the same. Fire people, well, they are a bright flash – here today, gone tomorrow. River folk, well, they tend to stay around a bit more. They continue, slowly moving throughout all, creating a path – quiet and humble. River folk provide the future for all, while the Fire people provide a flash in the night. Which one are you?"

In business, just like in nature, it is important for a leader to understand that long-term change requires patience, understanding and fortitude. Justice will prevail, the universe will balance. The law of nature is a law of duality, where light and darkness, good and evil, up and down, all work together to reach equilibrium. The scale will balance, but this is not in our control, we cannot force change.

Leaders must have an understanding of the impact of their actions – every choice, every decision, every day. There is an integral relationship between words and actions; our character is not something that we can hide. Our actions become our character. Leaders who understand this relationship quickly are able to make sound decisions and influence better outcomes.

Outstanding leaders share the knowledge that each individual choice they make will enable future outcomes, and not force them. They are cautious and calculated – looking at the long-term strategy rather than short-term gain.

Outstanding leaders understand that this requires diligence in decision-making, but they do not over manage. Instead, they are willing to accept that not every decision will have a favorable outcome. They are willing to quickly learn from failure. Learning from failure is a key step in growth; leaders never try to force success with every step.

In addition, outstanding leaders do not waste time protecting people from themselves. The universal scale will ensure the correct outcomes, and will manage to find the right amount of justice. There are no reasons for a strong leader to play favorites. This will actually have the opposite effect, by misaligning the underlying truth of universal balance – that all people are created equal. Where you may intend for someone to rise through the ranks, their lack of ability may cause you to work more hours cleaning up mistakes they make. Leaders recognize this relationship, and look to focus on leading with humility and understanding, rather than with favoritism.

Leadership is a responsibility; one that is greatly rewarding, but also humbling. It is important to understand that leadership does not mean dictating, commanding, and appointing, but instead leading from the rear.

Outstanding leaders understand that the long-term strategy of team development is more valuable than individual accolade. They focus on developing teams that can exceed expectations, through their own desires, wants, and needs – not in search of a feeling of superiority.

Outstanding leaders recognize the importance of individual contribution, but also see the difference between these individual successes and shared goals; team members must believe in the outcomes. Without group alignment, groupthink will fill the organization – and will present challenges to the ability to develop strong, high performing teams.

Outstanding leaders work to lead like water and not fire. They are focused on long-term impact, through gradual and continual guidance and support. They are able to adapt and work in any setting, flowing and permeating every aspect of an organization. These leaders are humble, yet strong; quiet yet roaring. They ebb and flow, adding value and strength where needed to accomplish the end goal.

Moving calmly between all things, the outstanding leader is a force that can be devastating if not properly channeled, but is constantly seeking to create the best path forward.

Like water, these leaders will constantly see, touch, and be present in the moment. There is a harmony with water, and an outstanding leader is similar, working to move forward ideas, teams, and projects. The outstanding leader continues involvement in all parts, good or bad, down the stream of delivery, until the successful end result is met.

Leaders Can Move On From the Past

Holding on can be the easiest thing to do. Letting go of control, leaving solid ground into the ocean of uncertainty is never easy. But we must know that there are other lands, other places we cannot see that exist beyond our understanding. Cast ashore in those places, and the journey begins.

The owner of a large and very successful lumber mill arrived at work one day to find a letter on his desk marked 'Urgent.' The postmark indicated it was from a competitor. He smiled and opened the letter, as if to indicate he already knew what it might say.

The letter read:

Dear Timberline Lumber Co.:

While you have been able to maintain a strong position in the market, we have recently created a new co-operation with all of the other lumber mills in the Midwest Valley.

This makes us the largest co-operation in the state.

Close down now.

Any workers who leave now will be provided work.

Sincerely,

J.T. Stillwater & Associates

The owner calmly placed the letter into the trashcan near his desk. He knew this day would come, so he was ready and prepared. He opened up his file cabinet, pulling out a dusty file from the very back. Blowing off the dust, he placed the manila folder on his desk. He opened up the folder, and began to read what was inside. Memories began to fill his mind, and he started to remember the next steps. He stood up, grabbed his jacket and headed out to the mill floor.

It was a good idea. The workers and management were already in an uproar. The letter had not only been delivered to him, but it was also distributed to the staff. As he walked across the mill yard, every eye was directly on him.

Attempting to exude confidence, but with a bit of fear, the owner grabbed a crate and placed it in the center of the group.

The owner stood on the box, placing his fingers to his mouth to whistle as loudly and shrilly as possible. Immediately, the murmurs ceased, and all was silent.

"Team," he explained. "I understand that many of you may have concerns with regard to recent developments. I am here to let you know that there is nothing to worry about." Reaching in the manila folder, he pulled out forms containing raises for each employee.

The faces in the yard were a look of shock and confusion. The owner knew he needed to act fast, so before anyone could muster the courage to ask questions, he asked them to take a walk out to the small lake that supplied water to the mill.

"Pay close attention," he stated, throwing a large piece of uncut lumber into the lake. The wood made a big splash as it landed in the water. The rough and uncut wood slowly began to bob up and down, circling in the middle of the lake. It didn't move much, but rather floated in the exact spot he had thrown it.

The group was huddled around the shoreline, straining and stretching to see the wood. But the owner could see that there was still much confusion. Sensing the lack of understanding, the owner then asked the group to follow him to the other side of the factory, where the river moved finished lumber to the docks for shipment.

"Again," he said, throwing a large piece of uncut lumber into the fast moving river, "observe." However, although the team watched as closely as humanly possible, there was still a look of confusion in their eyes. He decided to explain.

"Team," he started to explain, "The new co-operation is like the lake. They are big, wide and far reaching. But they cannot move a simple piece of lumber. We, on the other hand, are like the river. We are smaller, but we are all aligned in one direction – moving together as one unit. We are efficient and precise. Our ability far surpasses that of the new co-operation."

It was as if a light had lifted a dark cloud. The faces of the team changed from anger and confusion to commitment and excitement. The group smiled; cheered. There was a new motivation to be better, and to work harder than before. They quickly dispersed to spread the news that the company was not closing down now or ever.

The owner was able to let go of the emotion, and focus on the goal. He knew that the only way to share the power was to let go of his ability to control the other company – and focus on the things he could impact. It wasn't easy, but the owner had a plan and a strategy which aligned to motivate and inspire.

Had he dwelled on the negative he may have closed his business. Instead he viewed the letter as a tool to help motivate his team to accomplish bigger and better things. The owner was so thankful to J.T. Stillwater & Associates for the opportunity to motivate his team that he sent them a fruit basket.

Many characteristics of great leaders are outwardly facing. We make observations on how leaders interact with others, and this shapes our thoughts on a person's leadership capability. We often admire things like public speaking, composure under pressure, listening skills, etc., and view these things as measure ments of a leader's ability to translate vision to reality.

But often there are other key aspects of leadership which are not addressed in these outwardly facing traits. An example of one such trait (perhaps one of the most important and difficult to master) is the idea of 'letting go.' This simple concept can mean the difference between a leader's ability to be effective and constantly being at odds with outcomes. Once a leader learns to let go, he will be filled with everything.

Have you ever tried to impress someone, only to realize they were in fact turned off? Remember trying to rush and make green lights, but ending up hitting more red ones? A leader will realize that the best work is done when you let go of things that are out of your control, and simply focus on the things you can control.

Why is letting go so difficult? Well, for one thing it is considered by many as a sign of weakness. Oddly enough, once mastered, this can help propel you to a position of strength. Many times, when there is a void, nature will work to consume it with the best possible option.

Forcing the hand, driving the change will complete the necessary task – but often leaving much to be desired by the affected parties. Relax, trust that the dynamics are such that each part will strive to see success, and allow the necessary changes to happen around you. Once again, you can only control yourself… feel comfortable letting things outside your manageable ability go.

This can best be described as a paradox, conflicting views which require each other to sustain. An example would be the concept of Yin-Yang. Comprised of interwoven dark and light shapes, each part relies on the other – ending in a complete circle. Yin-Yang visualizes the concept that you must let go of total control to have any control; you give to become more. When you desire nothing, everything you desire will come. By letting go of certain things, a leader will benefit from filling these voids with the best possible options.

To be clear, letting go doesn't mean being immobile or unengaged. It doesn't mean throwing in the towel and walking away. There are different approaches to letting go. For some situations, it can be as simple as a calm or still moment of reflection. Taking a step back, ending a meeting, or grabbing an early lunch. Constant engagement is not always required.

A leader will learn that actions along with speech are very important tools. However, so is inaction and silence. Letting go can require a leader to teach through actions, rather than speech or engagement. Effectiveness through calculated thought, stillness and problem solving rather than constant chatter or ineffective meetings, are the key. Cooperation with all forces will allow the dynamics to perform at a high level.

Control has its place but remember to not take yourself too seriously. Command and control has a place – but it cannot be a constant process. Be smart; use it with tact and understanding. A well thought out pause or change will have a very strong impact.

Outstanding leadership is not only about the outwardly facing actions you make. Some of the leadership comes from inwardly facing skills. Release the desire for constant words and actions, release things you cannot change. Internal development will begin when you focus more energy and time on things you can change, can influence.

Our minds are very capable tools, but they do not like to squander processing power on irrelevant topics. This will simply be transformed into anxiety, stress, and failure. Let your brain power the thoughts and development as it wants, looking at the real problems and challenges you face as a leader.

Leaders Think and Act Accordingly

If we attempt to force change, we will succeed. We will inevitably change ourselves to become irrelevant. Change happens naturally, leaders are those who can help explain why.

In Egypt, along the Nile River, there was an old man who could no longer help build the pyramids. Instead, he spent his days gathering water for the fields and growing food for the workers.

In order to do so, he had developed a system of a pole with two pots which he carried on his back. Each pot contained water, and every day he would walk a path from the Nile to the field with the pots, delivering valuable water to the canals.

Over time, one of the pots developed a small leak, dripping water as he walked along the path to the river. The good pot was critical of the leaky pot and constantly pointed out his flaws. "You are a terrible pot. Everyday you leak water, and I have to make up the slack."

As time went on, the constant negative feedback began to wear on the leaky pot. It began to believe the narrative, and after much introspection, the broken pot realized what it must do.

"Master," the broken pot could barely speak, it was so upset. "I am sorry that I am broken and let you down." The broken pot continued.

"Each day as we walk the path to the river I cannot hold on to all the water you place in me. I spill out all over the place, and waste so much time and effort. I am not efficient, am a poor performer, and you must replace me. Replace me so you can be more successful!"

Hearing this, the old man was in shock. The old man realized the cracked pot did not fully understand its role. He quickly began to explain.

"Broken pot, you provide so many benefits to me that you do not realize! Did you notice all of the vegetables growing along your side of the path? I knew you dripped water and so I planted seeds along your side of our path. Your water nurtured those plants and vegetables. The other pot may seem more complete, but I would have to stop and tip it every time I wanted to give the plants a drink. Water flows from you perfectly!"

The broken pot smiled, and quickly went back to work – dripping water along the path.

Everyone has participated in some activity that he/she feels is a waste of time. We question the reasons for utilizing resources on a project or initiative that is dead. In our busy schedules, there are so many other tasks, duties, and important things to tend to, that we dread the idea of wasted time.

Outstanding leadership requires an objective awareness of what is happening. Understanding the dynamics of a group is important, but having a clear understanding of situational factors is imperative. When thinking about leadership, it is important to recognize that the specific actions a leader may take to impact a group can matter less than his/her ability to have an uncluttered view of the problems.

Action for action's sake may help the perception of progress; it may give some sense of immediate relief. But action without strategy around a solution is merely an action. We can see how this does not translate to better leadership or even better command and control. It becomes another stone in the canyon of mediocre management.

Outstanding leaders must be different; they must lead by providing crystal clear thought to existing problems as they arise, without an agenda. There can be no manipulation of the facts, and it must be fair and solution-based.

They must do what is right – focusing on the immediate opportunities and quick wins. Solution-based problem-solving for leaders is a learned skill, as it requires creativity, and outside the box thinking. But this is how you craft a leaky pot into a top performer.

Often, leaders fall into the pitfalls of 'solutions for now.' This involves making decisions that are based solely upon a 'should' vs. 'should not' equation. This rests entirely on the goals of an organization, regardless of outcomes. It sheds no light on what is actually going on, and will most likely end up clouding another leader's ability to make decisions.

Leaders, who lose sight of the truth of any situation, lose the ability to be agile. They gain the ability to do 'what is expected,' but lose any real leadership value in turn. The continued loss of real leadership ability begins to erode the overall productivity of the teams and organizations, resulting in an environment of coercion.

Oustanding leaders ensure that they process information from a state of clarity, and are not influenced. This results in decisions being recognized as legitimate and will produce better results over time.

Leaders Take No Sides

You may win an argument, but lose an ally. You may prove a point, but lose a friend. You may be the only one correct, but you will also be the only one.

On a giant plateau, high above the land below a teacher mentored a group of students in the art of leadership. It was a meager and humble existence; long days filled with quiet meditation. After some time, one by one, the students would leave the plateau to the valley below to share the wisdom they learned.

The teacher did not mandate how long students would study. Each student's journey was meant to be unique, and often students would leave after a short stay with little or no notice. It was not uncommon for new faces to come and go regularly during the course of a year.

Othe students stayed for several years. One of these students had been with the teacher for almost 6 years. After long years of dedicated practice, the student had still not learned the key to leadership – true enlightenment. This was difficult, as it was the student's only desire in life.

At the end of the sixth year, the teacher did something unprecedented. He gave the student an ultimatum. Complete the training, or seek enlightenment elsewhere. This was extremely difficult for the student to hear, but it made sense as this was the whole purpose of living in such a place for so long.

The student struggled for many long nights questioning his destiny. It was apparent that there could not be a 'forced awakening.' However, the student was determined to find true enlightenment – at any cost.

One day during meditation, a strong wind swept over the plateau. The trees in the courtyard shuddered in the violent wind, causing leaves to fall violently from the branches. One by one, the leaves swirled haphazardly, landing on the tiles that made up the courtyard floor.

The student had an epiphany. "I can no longer fight destiny. Like a falling leaf, I must follow my path to the ground gracefully." The student then committed to leave the teacher, descend the plateau, and live below in the valley, without the ever gaining true enlightenment.

The student was heartbroken, but knew it was important to share the decision with the teacher. As the student began to explain, the teacher quickly interrupted. With another unprecedented decision, the teacher, smiled and stated, "When you leave tomorrow, I will join you on your trip to the valley."

The student was in shock. This had never happened before, and the student wondered about the purpose. Did the teacher want to embarrass him for his lack of discipline? There were so many questions going through the student's mind. One thing was certain; the teacher had never made the descent with a student.

The next morning, before the two started the descent into the valley, the teacher paused for a second, and looked down from the high plateau to the valley down below. He looked for a moment, and then sighed. It was as if there was sadness at the upcoming departure. With a sweeping arm, the teacher pointed across the horizon, and asked the student to describe the sights.

Confused, the student said, "I see the sun gradually moving across the far mountains. I see hills covered with grass and trees. There is a small village next to a stream, and a crystal blue lake."

The teacher smiled, placing a hand on the student's shoulder, and gently motioned toward the path to the valley down the plateau. In silence they started the journey.

They walked without a word, not stopping for food or rest. After several long days of the journey, they approached the base of the plateau. Here, the teacher paused again, looking around at the scenery. The teacher asked the student to describe the sights once again.

"I see cows in meadows grazing, small homes, and children by the stream playing in the water."

Once more the teacher motioned for them to continue down the path. As the two of them walked toward the entrance of the village at the bottom of the plateau, the teacher stopped the student again.

"At this point the journey is complete. Tell me – what have you learned?" Caught off guard, the student had nothing to say.

After a long pause the teacher smiled. "There wasa reason you did not gain true enlightenment through your studies at the top of the plateau. All of the wisdom gained at the top of the plateau will not prepare one for life in the valley."

The teacher continued, and the student listened closely. "All of my past students have failed to learn this valuable lesson. They believed that the knowledge gained at the top would help them understand those down below – when in reality it is just the opposite. In your journey, you learned that a single point of view only teaches one way of thinking. Sometimes understanding requires seeing things from all perspectives."

With closed eyes, the student sighed a breath of relief – it all made sense. As he opened his eyes to express his thanks, he found that he was alone at the gate to the village.

Outstanding leaders are often pull the best from within people. Often, this requires tough conversations and blunt honesty. These can result in heated conversations, arguments, and even hurt feelings. As a leader, it can be difficult to maintain a positive focus when challenging or being challenged.

While the 'Command and Control' approach has its place, outstanding leaders who can collaboratively manage through conflict will often ensure future success by building trust and strong relationships. This can come in the form of establishing clarity of thought – focusing on the goals rather than personal agendas or recognition. Clarity will also come from understanding that being 'right' is not always right.

Often, leaders will need to take things a step further. On the battlefield, generals will frequently yield a strategic position in order to win. In business, like in battle, being graceful and yielding your position can lead to a positive outcome. This will allow you to regain control of the things you can manage, and tactfully return to facilitating what is actually happening.

As a leader, there is never a benefit to winning an argument, or proving that you are right. There is never a good reason to point out the flaws in the arguments or ideas of others. An outstanding leader should never harbor feelings of resentment or insecurity if another's approach is utilized; even if it leads to an unsatisfactory outcome.

Everyone must learn, and sometimes this lesson is required to ensure future success. A leader should be able to focus with clarity on the bigger picture, and remember that there are greater and more strategic goals at play. One decision, mistake, or wrong turn should never create enough chaos to upset a strategic outcome.

An outstanding leader can view all sides of the equation together, and align sights onfuture outcomes. Remembering that not every team member has a direct line of sight to the organizational goals, an outstanding leader recognizes that it can be difficult for team members to always make the best decision.

It is more important that they make decisions, accept responsibility, and learn from their mistakes than it is for them to be perfect. For a leader, it is the focus on the flow, and keeping things moving in a positive direction. A leader should be able to engage with the water of delivery without making waves around the execution of the plan.

This is a key point. Outstanding leaders should try to emulate the strength and resilience of water. As water flows, it is fluid, soft, and yielding. But water will wear away a canyon, which is both rigid and unyielding. A leader, like water, should calmly guide and let the flow happen – trying to stop it will only make matters worse.

Instead, view the flow from different angles, and work to understand why it is taking the path. Just like water, it may rush to that which provides least resistance. However, it can often crash through barriers and knock down levies. It really depends on the goal – where does it want to end up?

As a leader, it can be challenging to understand the viewpoints of others. In order to be successful, this is a critical skill. Having tough conversations, encouraging innovation, and challenging the status quo are great – but remember to adhere to the principle of water. Let the flow happen; allow the different ideas to surface. If not, you are a rigid element and will break over time.

By taking no sides and allowing the flow to occur, you and your team will become stronger.

Leaders See a Vision Which is Hidden to Others

Blind faith exists in rare situations. In most cases, people believe in things that are tangible. The creative process involves complexities of new thought, thereby creating a natural sense of fear for those who cannot see.

In a time when lands were still ruled by Kings and Queens, there was a humble farmer who worked a small plot of land. The farmer loved his land, and found great pleasure in providing fresh fruits and vegetables to the local community. He was well versed in the art of farming, and there was never a season where he didn't have a bountiful harvest.

Every spring he would plant seeds, carefully looking after them, providing water and plenty of sunlight, and waiting for them to break out of the soil. In the fall the farmer was rewarded for his hard work with a bountiful harvest. As winter settled into the land, the farmer would enjoy stores of dried vegetables and fruits, and calmly wait for another spring.

The farmer was a good, kind soul. He understood that there were others who did not always fare as well as he did. He made a point to share his harvest with those around him. Every year, people would come from far and wide to share his harvest. They were always grateful, and never took more than what the farmer could offer.

One afternoon, as the farmer was working his land, he heard the sound of a horse approaching. Placing his tools aside, he stopped working to see who was arriving. It was a knight in full armor riding under the King's crest. This meant the visit was official business, so the farmer immediately stood at attention. The knight quickly dismounted, and walked over to the farmer with his hand outstretched in friendship.

"Farmer," said the knight, "I come bearing news from the King. He requests your presence at the castle."

The farmer was shocked, but excited. It was a great honor to meet the King. Not taking a moment to ask why, the farmer immediately gathered his belongings, and prepared for the journey to meet the King.

As the two set off to the castle, the knight reminded the farmer that the journey was long, and had many dangers along the way. "Have no fear, farmer. I will protect you."

After many long days of riding, the pair began to enter a dark wooded area. It was said that the area was home to evil spirits. "Carry on, farmer. I will protect you from any evil spirits," exclaimed the knight.

At that moment, before the two could take another step, a witch appeared in front of them.

"Who dares to enter my woods?" she cackled. The knight quickly responded, "Move aside! I am taking this man to see the King."

The witch laughed. "Your King has no rule of my woods, and I do not appreciate your tone. What a great pair of toads you will be." The witch started to swing her wand in the direction of the travelers, but she stopped abruptly looking directly at the farmer. "Wait… farmer, is that you?"

"Yes, I am on my way to see the king," the farmer replied.

"Farmer," said the witch, "Last year you provided me some of your harvest for my potions. It was generous and kind; my thanks is your safe passage." The farmer and knight quickly continued down the path and out of the woods without looking back.

After a couple days, they reached a very large river crossing. The King had built a bridge over the river, but with recent rains it had washed out. Instead of a bridge, a ferryman stood watch to move people and cargo across to the other side. It was rumored that the ferryman did not like the King, and would not help any of the King's men across.

"Knight," said the ferryman, "I hope that you are not planning on crossing here. I have issue with the King, and will not help any of his men.

Two days walk from here the river is calm, I suggest you head that way."

The Knight unsheathed his sword, "Like it or not, you must oblige. I am on official business." This caused others around to take notice, and a small group of merchants waiting to cross had started to gather.

"I think you would do best to move on." The ferryman held a pole, and the small crowd started to surround the pair. The knight was ready to fight.

Then, the ferryman dropped his pole and walked directly towards the farmer.

"Good sir, good sir! I had no idea it was you," he shouted, "Please farmer, for all you have done for my family – this ferry ride is free!"

The group quickly loaded the knight and the farmer's gear onto the ferry. Within minutes, the two had been shuttled to the other side of the river, and were on their way.

Once across the river, it was a short distance to the castle, and the two arrived in no time. The Knight proceeded to present the farmer to the King, "King, I present you the farmer."

"Ahhh," said the King, "I welcome you to my castle, but I regret it is in sorrow instead of joy." The King went on to explain.

"Farmer, we are at war. A great land to the north filled with our enemies has invaded, and is moving our way. I cannot fight the enemy, but I have a solution. I have commanded my troops to take wood from the enchanted forest, and build a dam over the great river. When the enemy approaches, we will remove the dam and sweep them all away." The farmer nodded in agreement. "This is a great plan...what troubles you?"

The King continued, "I have ordered my troops to the forest, but they keep coming back as toads. That witch has not followed my orders to evacuate. Then, we attempted to start building a dam, but the ferryman and his gang continue to disobey my orders and destroy anything we build." The farmer understood the problem, but still was confused as to his role.

"I can imagine you are wondering why you are here?" the King smiled. "Farmer, I have sent for hundreds of people from all over the land. Each one had a knight for protection. You are the only one who has made it to me. The knight told me that every time your life was in peril, the people were thankful and offered you safe passage. I must understand why."

"King," said the farmer, "I am a simple man. I take joy in working my land, and every year, when my harvest is bountiful I share my blessings. King, you are a great man. You take joy in owning the land, but every year, when our harvest is bountiful; you tax the people."

The King looked confused, so the farmer paused for a moment. And then the farmer had an idea on how to convey his message a different way.

"King, in order to have a bountiful harvest, I must obey the Sun. It dictates the seasons, and in this way my harvest also. I owe my livelihood to it. But, as great as it is, the sun offers its sunlight for free. It gives it away every morning for all who wake to see. And over time, my seeds all reach toward the sun. From its offering of light, the seeds grow strong and tall. They grow upward, striving to be close to the sun. Perhaps, you could be more like the sun."

"This is the most insane idea I have ever heard, but thank you for the laugh!" exclaimed the King. "Give this man a bag of gold for his trouble, and be on your way." The King continued to laugh as the farmer, gold in hand, left the castle.

The next spring, the enemy troops advanced, overthrowing the King and his castle was destroyed. The farmer continued to farm his land and share his bountiful harvest every season.

There are two kinds of leaders. The first kind of leader learns why negative things happen and manages accordingly. The second kind of leader learns how negative things happen, but simply doesn't care. Don't be the second kind.

The second leader is one who focuses on outward praise. Such leaders seek recognition for actions, rather than skill. They are constantly working to impress, and sell themselves as experts, rather than allowing an organic growth of recognition to take place.

They are usually very ineffective, and are typically not held in high regard by the teams they support. They will obtain kudos in public venues, but be ridiculed behind closed doors.

The second leader is one in transition. At times, such leaders may understand how things are working, and be able to successfully and clearly influence decisions – but they can also forget and lead teams into disarray.

These leaders may continue to slide back into their past behavior, rather than learn from the past and move forward. These repeated mistakes are usually costly and time-consuming. The good news is that these leaders are usually a simple step away from being the first kind of leader.

The most desirable type of leader, is one that can adjust, adapt, and learn from mistakes. These leaders are not infallible, they make mistakes like anyone. But the difference is how they manage to learn through their mistakes. They take input, feedback and insight – always wondering "How can I be better?"

They do not possess any magical mirror to predict the future, but they seem to make lasting and impactful change with little or no effort. These leaders are flexible and fluid like water, and they accept that the only thing constant in life is change. They focus on the flow, and moving things forward toward common goals.

An outstanding leader shows allegiance only to the learning from mistakes – understanding how and why certain things happen. An outstanding leader has allegiance to the team – to ensure that the team is successful and can move things forward. An outstanding leader has a duty. Becoming a better leader can and will inspire others to achieve. This self reflection and motivation is critical for teams, organizations, and companies to be successful. Greatness encourages greatness.

Leaders Help the Group Synergy

'A process will develop over time. Actions will create reaction, and as they do, patterns will emerge from the process. Our inputs are actions, but the process is our understanding of the relationship between these actions and the outcomes. You cannot have one without the other'

A large law firm had a staff of well-trained paralegals. This team was very punctual, never made mistakes, and was known as on of the best in the city. It was one of the reasons the firm had been so successful.

One day the company installed a new printer. This printer was important to the firm, as it helped the paralegals print all of the documents required for court cases.

During the first week, the paralegals noticed that the printer made an awful sound when it printed documents. This loud and obnoxious drone could be heard all the way to the Board room, and several attorneys had complained about the noise during client meetings.

One of the paralegals noticed that if you jumped up, you could see the Board room down the hall, and determine if there were any meetings taking place. This way you could print the documents without disturbing any meetings. So, all the paralegals would quickly jump up, and check for meetings prior to printing any documents.

When a new paralegal joined the team, they noticed the jumping ritual and followed suit, jumping prior to printing a document. It seemed like an odd practice, but since everyone was doing it, the new hire wanted to fit in and get things right, since this was one of the elite firms in the city.

Over time, as one junior paralegal would join, another senior paralegal would leave. Eventually, there was an entirely new paralegal staff in the office. But the jumping tradition continued. Each new paralegal, unaware of the reason, would jump prior to printing a document.

The Board room was eventually moved to another floor, and the paralegals were left alone. But the jumping and printing became a standard regimen. Even though they did not know why, all the new paralegals kept jumping and printing. They had all learned the concept of status quo. We do it that way because that's how it's always been done.

Group processes emerge and evolve naturally. Groups are usually very self-regulating, despite your input, feedback, and will. In general, efforts to control the group dynamic will fail, so it is better to trust in the now, and understand the aspects of what is happening. If there is conflict, understand why. If there is synergy, understand why.

Is the group struggling to reach consensus? Is the group upset? Are there problems you cannot solve? It's ok! You won't be able to fix the issues, and even if you could, your involvement may well deprive the group of the creative process – eliminating crucial innovation along the way.

As a leader, allow the process to happen. It will unfold, and rather than rail against it – facilitate. Be calm, collected, and focused on the vision. Remember the reasons the group formed, and encourage all things you control that will help that end result.

As a leader, if you can explain the 'why' something happens, you are much more valuable to the team than someone who can simply manage a process that is going to happen anyway.

Rather than force change, allow the group to adapt. Most likely, if the team sees a leader that can move things forward in a clear and practical manner, it will attempt to adapt to your processes and behaviors. It is not human nature to repeat failed processes that generate poor results. In general, although we seek the path of least resistance, we also strive to survive, and mistakes do not equal survival.

Remember that processes develop over time, and the best pactices will eventually rise to the top – regardless of your feedback. As a leader, showing, rather than telling is the best option.

Exude confidence, clarity of thought, and decision-making.

Over time, allowing the process to develop naturally will ultimately encourage people and give validation to your leadership capabilities.

Growth as a Leader

W hen provided with a hard, cold, and seemingly lifeless seed it can be difficult to imagine that contained within are the makings of a beautiful plant, tree, or flower. From the outside, there is little indication of that potential. This is how nature works. Our natural world is not designed to provide all of the answers upfront. Our world is designed to share a journey, a transformation, and the experience.

Add water, soil, and sun to the seed, and over time it will grow. As it grows, there are small indications of the future. Perhaps a small bulb will appear – a leaf. These are signs of the future – the glory to come. But the consistent water, soil, and sun are still required. If these let up at any time, the process will fail.

With time, the plant grows strong. It now has leaves and blossoms. The flower is found, but only after taking the time and necessary care to ensure that the process was followed. The dedication, follow-up and hope of the future are rewarded with one of nature's most amazing creations.

This book is not intended to be a one-stop solution. Rather, the book should inspire you to continue along a path of self-discovery. The stories that you have just read should provide guidance as you continue to develop and hone your leadership skills. Refer to them often, when in doubt and presented with a challenge. The guidance and wisdom does not expire. Use these tools as a framework as you become an outstanding leader.

I hope that this work has provided you with some insight into different ways to approach leadership. There is a great leader in each of us. We are all at different stages, moving in different directions, but all intertwined in this great event of life.

Outstanding leaders relate to that connection, and find ways to align themselves and the situations they are in to move in a successful direction.

The fire, passion and focus you feel about becoming a better leader is felt by many just like you. I say this not to minimize your own personal journey, but to assure you that you are not alone. At any given moment, someone somewhere is wondering how to become a better leader. Share as you learn; and grow.

Remember, it is not the journey of an individual – but one of a whole. Embrace the challenges and share in the experience. Never be afraid to unleash the outstanding leader within.

NOTES

NOTES

NOTES

NOTES

NOTES

NOTES

NOTES

NOTES

NOTES

NOTES

NOTES

NOTES

NOTES

NOTES

NOTES

NOTES

NOTES

NOTES

NOTES

NOTES

NOTES

NOTES

NOTES

NOTES

NOTES

NOTES

NOTES

NOTES

NOTES

www.ingramcontent.com/pod-product-compliance
Lightning Source LLC
Chambersburg PA
CBHW051432090426
42737CB00014B/2929